AUSTRALIAN JOURNEY

Outback

Debra Doenges & Andrew Teakle

NEW HOLLAND

Dedication

This book is dedicated to Robert and Noela Teakle. Your love, patience, gentle guidance and understanding have made my journey through life so full of joy and adventure. Being blessed with the most wonderful parents is the greatest gift imaginable.

First published in Australia in 2009 by
New Holland Publishers (Australia) Pty Ltd
Sydney • Auckland • London • Cape Town

www.newholland.com.au

1/66 Gibbes Street Chatswood NSW 2067 Australia
218 Lake Road Northcote Auckland New Zealand
86 Edgware Road London W2 2EA United Kingdom
80 McKenzie Street Cape Town 8001 South Africa

National Library of Australia Cataloguing-in-Publication Data:

Australian journey : Outback / photographers Debra Doenges and Andrew Teakle.

9781741108170 (hbk.)

Photography, Artistic.
Australia, Central--Pictorial works.

Doenges, Debra.
Teakle, Andrew.

919.42

Publisher: Fiona Schultz
Publishing manager: Lliane Clarke
Designer: Domenika Fairy
Production manager: Olga Dementiev
Printer: SNP/Leefung Printing Co. Ltd (China)

Cover: Uluṟu and Honey Grevillea, Uluṟu-Kata Tjuṯa National Park, NT, Andrew Teakle

Title Page: Sacred Kingfisher, Kakadu National Park, NT, Andrew Teakle

Page 3: Bungle Bungles in morning light, Purnululu National Park, WA, Andrew Teakle

Page 4: Bottle Trees near Longreach, Qld, Andrew Teakle

INTRODUCTION

The Australian Outback is often seen as the lifeless wasteland depicted in the Mad Max movies: devoid of natural beauty and inhabited only by the roughest loners of society. Of course, this is far from the truth. The Outback is vast (some 70 per cent of the entire continent is considered arid) and at first glance appears lifeless. It is only when you really peer into the land that you see the signs of life: an incredibly well-camouflaged lizard blending into the rock upon which it suns itself; the circling speck of a black kite patrolling the landscape for carrion…or a sunbathing lizard; a kangaroo blending into the tawny tussocks of spiny grass, seeking the meagre shelter of a stunted gumtree. When you peer even further, you'll see tracks in the sand: the footsteps of the complex dance that occurs every night in this arid landscape.

It is at night that the desert comes alive. Insects, reptiles and marsupials emerge from their subterranean homes after the deadly sting of the sun has abated. They scurry in the frantic race to find food or a mate, to escape from predators, and to make it back to their burrows before the morning shift clocks on.

You don't have to be a naturalist, though, to appreciate the wonder of the Outback. Within the interior of Australia are landscapes to make the best-travelled visitor stop in amazement. The shape of Uluru from a distance is so familiar it has become almost cliché, yet to stand just beside this towering monolith is an exercise in humility. Its vastness and the incredible sense of timelessness one feels in its presence are overwhelming. Just 40 kilometres away are the arguably more spectacular Kata Tjuta. Known for many years by European Australians as the Olgas, the domes of this complex conceal secret hideaways, many of which have spiritual significance to their indigenous owners.

In this book, we will show you the best of Australia's mighty Outback. From Darwin, we head into Western Australia through the Kimberley and down into the red rock gorges of the Pilbara. Back into the Northern Territory, the journey continues through the heart of Australia and down to Lake Eyre and the Flinders Ranges. We'll then head north up the Birdsville Track to the spectacular dunes of the Simpson Desert and continue to Queensland's Gulf Country.

I hope you enjoy your journey through this vast and enigmatic heart of Australia.

Andrew Teakle

Sunset over Fannie Bay
Darwin, NT

Andrew Teakle

Dawn at Fannie Bay
Darwin, NT

Andrew Teakle

Smith Street Mall
Darwin, NT

Andrew Teakle

Parliament House
Darwin, NT

Andrew Teakle

Sunset from Ubirr
Kakadu National Park, NT

Andrew Teakle

Nourlangie rock art
Kakadu National Park, NT

Andrew Teakle

Saltwater crocodile
Kakadu National Park, NT

Andrew Teakle

Sea Eagle at nest
Kakadu National Park, NT

Andrew Teakle

Jim Jim Falls
Kakadu National Park, NT

Andrew Teakle

View from Ubirr
Kakadu National Park, NT

Andrew Teakle

Magela Wetlands
Kakadu National Park, NT

Andrew Teakle

Magela Wetlands
Kakadu National Park, NT

Andrew Teakle

Melaleucas on Yellow Waters
Kakadu National Park, NT

Andrew Teakle

Park management using fire
Kakadu National Park, NT

Andrew Teakle

Tolmer Falls
Litchfield National Park, NT

Debra Doenges

Wangi Falls
Litchfield National Park, NT

Andrew Teakle

Magnetic termite mounds
Litchfield National Park, NT

Debra Doenges

Blyth Homestead
Litchfield National Park, NT

Andrew Teakle

Cascade and potholes
Nitmiluk National Park, N

Andrew Teakle and
Debra Doenges

Canoeing Katherine Gorge
Nitmiluk National Park, NT

Andrew Teakle and Debra Doenges

Afternoon glow
Keep River National Park, N

Debra Doenges

Boab and vine
Keep River National Park, NT

Debra Doenges

28

Aboriginal rock art
Keep River National Park, NT

Debra Doenges and Andrew Teakle

Sandstone formations
Keep River National Park, NT

Andrew Teakle

Hidden Valley
Mirima National Park, WA

Andrew Teakle

Hidden Valley
Mirima National Park, WA

Andrew Teakle

Cane grass hillside
East Kimberley, WA

Andrew Teakle

Sunset over Cambridge Gulf
Wyndham, WA

Andrew Teakle

Marglu Billabong
Parry Lagoon Nature Reserve, WA

Andrew Teakle

Marglu Billabong
Parry Lagoon Nature Reserve, WA

Debra Doenges

Boab in fog
Parry Lagoon Nature Reserve, WA

Debra Doenges

Waterbirds in morning fog
Parry Lagoon Nature Reserve, WA

Andrew Teakle

38

Boabs and wireless station
Parry Lagoon Nature
Reserve, WA

Debra Doenges

Zebedee Springs
El Questro Station, WA

Debra Doenges

Froghole loop
Purnululu National Park, WA

Andrew Teakle

Beehive domes
Purnululu National Park, WA

Debra Doenges

Silhouette in Froghole Gorge
Purnululu National Park, WA

Andrew Teakle

Bungle Bungles in morning light
Purnululu National Park, WA

Debra Doenges

Bungle Bungles
Purnululu National Park, WA

Andrew Teakle

Termite mound
Purnululu National Park, WA

Debra Doenges

46

Afternoon light on Gantheaume Point
Broome, WA

Debra Doenges

Honeycomb rock at Gantheaume Point
Broome, WA

Debra Doenges

Snappy Gum
Karijini National Park, WA

Debra Doenges

Oxers Lookout
Karijini National Park, WA

Debra Doenges

Cascade in Dales Gorge
Karijini National Park, WA

Debra Doenges

Fortesque Falls
Karijini National Park, WA

Andrew Teakle

Snappy Gum overlooking Dales Gorge
Karijini National Park, WA

Andrew Teakle

Handrail Gorge
Karijini National Park, WA

Andrew Teakle

Last light
Devils Marbles Conservation Reserve, NT

Andrew Teakle

Ghost Gum
Devils Marbles Conservation Reserve, NT

Andrew Teakle

Cleaved boulder
Devils Marbles Conservation Reserve, NT

Debra Doenges

Stepping stones
Devils Marbles Conservation
Reserve, NT

Debra Doenges

58

Wedge-tailed Eagle
Alice Springs Desert Park, NT

Andrew Teakle

Sturt's Desert Pea
Alice Springs, NT

Andrew Teakle

Palm Valley
Finke Gorge National Park, NT

Andrew Teakle

Ghost Gum
Finke Gorge National Park, NT

Debra Doenges

Spinifex and Ruby Dock
Finke Gorge National Park, NT

Debra Doenges

Ruby Dock and Ptilotis
Finke Gorge National
Park, NT

Andrew Teakle

Afternoon light
Finke Gorge National Park, NT

Andrew Teakle

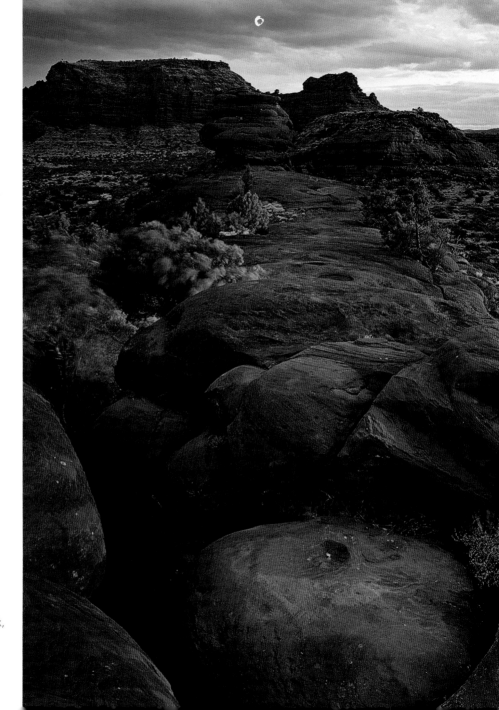

Kalaranga Lookout
Finke Gorge National Park,
NT

Debra Doenges

Palm Valley rockpool
Finke Gorge National Park, NT

Andrew Teakle

Riverside campground
Finke Gorge National Park, NT

Andrew Teakle

Chain of hollows
Uluṟu-Kata Tjuṯa
National Park, NT

Andrew Teakle

Uluru and Honey Grevillea
Uluru-Kata Tjuta
National Park, NT

Andrew Teakle

Senna and Grevillea around Uluṟu
Uluṟu-Kata Tjuṯa National Park, NT

Andrew Teakle

Honey Grevillea
and Native Bee
Uluru-Kata Tjuta
National Park, NT

Andrew Teakle

Boulder and flowering Mul
Uluṟu-Kata Tjuṯa
National Park, NT

Debra Doenges

Rain streaks on Uluṟu
Uluṟu-Kata Tjuṯa
National Park, NT

Debra Doenges

Uluṟu silhouette at dawn
Uluṟu-Kata Tjuṯa National Park, NT

Debra Doenges

Storm clouds build over Kata Tjuṯa
Uluṟu-Kata Tjuṯa National Park, NT

Debra Doenges

Dawn silhouette
Uluru-Kata Tjuṯa National Park, NT

Andrew Teakle

Kings Canyon
Watarrka National Park, NT

Andrew Teakle

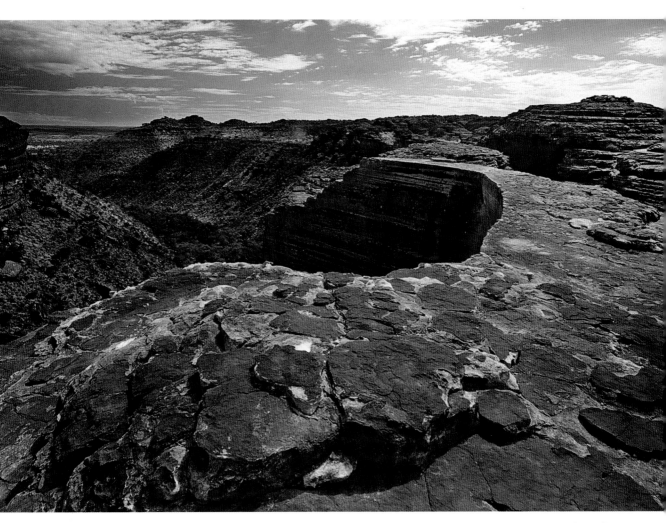

Kings Canyon
Watarrka National Park, NT

Andrew Teakle

Pioneer Bridge
Watarrka National Park, NT

Debra Doenges

Perentie sunbathing
Watarrka National Park, NT

Andrew Teakle

Kings Canyon wall
Watarrka National Park, NT

Debra Doenges

Cycad in the Garden of Eden
Watarrka National Park, NT

Debra Doenges

Ptilotis after summer rains
Mereenie Loop, NT

Andrew Teakle

Spring wildflowers
Mereenie Loop, NT

Andrew Teakle

Outback sunset
Stuart Highway, SA

Andrew Teakle

Ruby Dock
Anna Creek, SA

Debra Doenges

Desert life
Lake Eyre National Park, SA

Andrew Teakle

Salt flats after water recedes
Lake Eyre National Park, SA

Debra Doenges

Banded Stilts at sunrise
Lake Eyre National Park, SA

Andrew Teakle

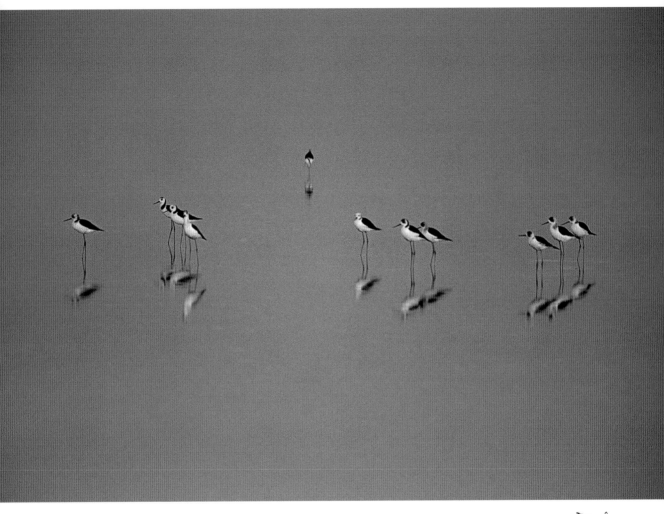

Banded Stilts
Lake Eyre National Park, SA

Debra Doenges

Saint Mary's Peak
Flinders Ranges National Park, SA

Andrew Teakle and Debra Doenges

92

View from Stokes Hill
Flinders Ranges National Park, SA

Debra Doenges

Bunyeroo Valley
Flinders Ranges National Park, SA

Andrew Teakle

Emu
Mount Remarkable National Park, SA

Andrew Teakle

Pioneer homestead and almond trees
Flinders Ranges, SA

Andrew Teakle

Onion weed and River Red Gums
Flinders Ranges, SA

Debra Doenges

Arkaroo rock art
Flinders Ranges, SA

Andrew Teakle and Debra Doenges

Dawn over dunes
Innamincka Nature Reserve, SA

Andrew Teakle

Corellas in flight
Innamincka Nature Reserve, SA

Andrew Teakle

Emus on the Birdsville Track
Sturt Stony Desert, SA

Andrew Teakle

Morning light on dune
Simpson Desert
National Park, Qld

Andrew Teakle

Sand dune detail
Simpson Desert
National Park, Qld

Andrew Teakle

Flowers on dune
Simpson Desert
National Park, Qld

Andrew Teakle

Cormorants
Birdsville Billabong, Qld

Andrew Teakle

White-plumed
Honeyeater
Birdsville Billabong, Qld

Andrew Teakle

Birdsville Hotel
Birdsville, Qld

Andrew Teakle

108

Moss garden
Canarvon Gorge
National Park, Qld

Andrew Teakle

Tree ferns in Ward's Canyon
Canarvon Gorge National Park, Qld

Andrew Teakle

Cycad frond
Canarvon Gorge
National Park, Qld

Andrew Teakle

The Amphitheatre
Canarvon Gorge
National Park, Qld

Debra Doenges
and Andrew Teakle

Aboriginal rock art
Canarvon Gorge National Park, Qld

Andrew Teakle

Life in the gorge
Canarvon Gorge National Park, Qld

Andrew Teakle and Debra Doenges

Ghungalu art site
Blackdown Tableland
National Park, Qld

Andrew Teakle

Rock Pools
Blackdown Tableland
National Park, Qld

Debra Doenges

Windmill at first light
Longreach, Qld

Andrew Teakle

Stockman's Hall of Fame
Longreach, Qld

Andrew Teakle

Flocking Corellas
Longreach, Qld

Andrew Teakle

Morning roost
Longreach, Qld

Andrew Teakle

South celestial pole
Bladensburg National Park, Qld

Andrew Teakle

Kangaroos on the hop
Bladensburg National Park, Qld

Andrew Teakle

Galahs
Bladensburg National Park, Qld

Andrew Teakle

Dusk settles
Bladensburg National Park, Qld

Andrew Teakle

Sunrise behind Mesa
Near Winton, Qld

Andrew Teakle
and Debra Doenges

125

Thunderbird fossil
Riversleigh, Qld

Andrew Teakle
and Debra Doenges

Lower Lawn Hill Gorge from Island Stack
Boodjamulla National Park, Qld

Andrew Teakle and Debra Doenges

Canoeing on Lawn Hill Creek
Boodjamulla National Park, Qld

Andrew Teakle and Debra Doenges

128

Waterlilies on
James River
Avon Downs, NT

Andrew Teakle